PRAYER COMPASS FOR VICTORY

TERRIFIC BIBLICAL PRAYER POINTS FOR TRIUMPH AND GLORY

Samuel Jimson Olorunfemi

Author of fast selling

Quiet Time,

Breaking the Evil Blood Covenant,

Prayer Pattern for Conquest

GOD'S TRIUMPHANT FAITH PUBLICATIONS

Published by

God's Triumphant Faith Publications
God's Greatness Plaza
AnuOluwa Estate, Alapo, Olorunda-Abaa
After Akobo-Ojurin Bus Stop, Akobo,
Ibadan, Oyo State, Nigeria, West Africa
Box 21281, U.I. Post Office, Ibadan
E-mail: sajorev7@yahoo.com
Tel: + 234 803 562 4406
+ 234 805 530 1639
+ 234 806 637 1796

First published 2016
Reprint, 2020

ISBN 979-8846440029

MAILING ADDRESS
Rev (Barrister) Samuel Jimson Olorunfemi
Box 21281, U.I. Post Office, Ibadan
Oyo State, Nigeria, West Africa
Tel: +234 803 562 4406
+234 805 530 1639
E-mail: sajorev7@yahoo.com

Unless otherwise specified, the Biblical quotations in this book are from the King James Version of the Holy Bible.

Contents

Dedication

Unto the Most High God, the Man of war, who has respect unto His covenant and as such always leads us in triumphal procession in Christ, over the dark places of the earth, that are full of the habitation of cruelty; and through us, spreads everywhere the fragrance of knowledge of Him. And we boldly say unto God ***"How terrible are you in your works! through the greatness of your power shall your enemies submit themselves unto you" (Psm. 66:3).***

Preface

Oh You God who hears prayer, to You shall all flesh come (Psalm 65:2).

Our God, the Creator of heavens and earth, the Almighty, is ***a prayer-answering God.*** He ***answers the prayers*** of His children – You and I, ***by fearful and glorious things that terrify the wicked, but makes the godly sing praises*** (Psalm 65: 5).

This prayer-answering God, by His might has founded the mountains, being girded with power. He stills the roaring of the seas, the roaring of their waves and the tumult of the peoples; so that those who dwell in earths's farthest part are afraid at nature's signs of His presence. This God is the only entity who has the audacity and temerity to declaratively say:

> ***". . . call on me in the day of trouble; I will deliver you, and ye shall honour and glorify me"*** (Psalm 50: 15).

The readiness of God to make you victorious in all battles of life is revealed by the following scriptural injunction which says:

> ***"The Lord shall fight for you and ye shall hold your peace and remain at rest"*** (Exodus 14:14 Amplified Bible).

It is also imperative to state that every page of this ***"prayer compass for victory"*** is ***saturated*** with Bible-based and Holy Ghost power packed prayer points that will translate you from an experiential position of: ***failure to success; bondage to freedom; hatred to being loved; ill-favour to favour; fear to faith; timidity to boldness; discouragement to courage; poverty to riches; lack and want***

to abundance; foolishness to wisdom; confusion to direction; impotency to potency; unrighteousness to righteousness; tail to headship. They have the potency to catapult you from the floor to the mountain's top.

Dear reader, with the aforesaid in view, my sincere advice for you is to make use of this instrument for victorious prayer with fervency and business-like-faith. Avoid distraction of any form by conscientiously study the inherent prayer points vis-a-vis the scriptural passages given. As you do these, I have no doubt that your misery shall turn to mastery; your mountainous challenges shall depart; the hills shall be removed, but God's covenant of peace shall never depart from you. I, therefore, welcome you to your haven of triumph, rejoicing and fulfillment where you shall have every cause to: ***"Say to God, How awesome and fearfully glorious (terrible) are Your works! Through the greatness of your power shall your enemies submit themselves to You (with feigned and reluctant obedience)" (Psm. 66:3, Ampl/KJV).***

Rev. Barrister Samuel Jimson Olorunfemi

Opening Testimony of Victory Via Prayer

Sometime in the month of May, 2012, I attended a Landlords' Association Meeting of my Estate, where I held my view and made some anomalous observation known before all the people that were present at the meeting. To my chagrin, suddenly, unwarranted violent reactions came from two among the people at the meeting against me. One of the attackers, who is a woman descended so much on me with rain of abuses and disparaging words. Her actions indicated that she had been appointed in the midst of some landlords who had held a secret meeting before that of the fateful morning's against me and my family. For no offence, she was given mandate to confront me the way she did, and the meeting closed on that note.

Nevertheless, each time the woman passed by me thereafter, she would utter one statement of abuse or curses to my hearing which I kept deaf ear to. She also frequently visited a particular house, which is the meeting point where they conspired against me and my family, with obvious acts to show that she and her co-conspirators are against me and my family.

Without being perturbed, I only reported the matter to God in prayer and declared evil to go back upon the sender. The good news is that the same woman suddenly became a victim of casualty. She was hit on one of her feet by a car being driven by a learner, which resulted in her broken foot and was thereafter rushed to a University Teaching Hospital as an orthopaedic patient.

Nonetheless, her major conspirator physically moved himself and every member of his family out of his own house without notice, to an unknown location in the same city, while his house has been left desolate for a period of 5 years, hitherto to align with God's word that says: **it shall not be well with the wicked.**

This is how God intervenes in the affairs of His children who trust in Him and sincerely call upon Him in prayers. Glory! Helleluyah!!

CHAPTER ONE

Entrance Into God's Presence

It is imperative to start this victorious prayer exercise by following the triumphant rules as biblically prescribed.

In other words, it is incumbent on us and also inevitable for us to begin on this triumphant prayer journey with thanksgiving and praise.

> ***"Enter into His gates with thanksgiving, And into His Courts with praise. Be thankful to Him, and bless His name"*** (Psalm 100:4, New King James Version).

THANKSGIVING

"Oh give thanks to the Lord, for He is good, because His mercy endures forever" (Psalm 118:1, 106:1).

"Oh give thanks to the Lord! Call upon His name; Make known His deeds among the people" (Psalm 105:1).

Beloved, one of the pre-requisites to gaining entrance into the gates of the Most High God is by giving Him thanks. God is indeed worthy of our (your) thanks-giving, because He is good and ever good to us (you) and His mercies endure for ever. Innumerable are reasons for which we have no option than to give thanks to God. Among them are the following:

1. For preserving us (you) spirit, soul and body alive and in Him.

2. For preserving every member of your (our) family (ies) alive.
3. For preserving every of your loved ones alive, be it in the church, in the neighbourhood, at work and in the secular world generally.

   "It is because of the LORD's mercies that we are not consumed, because His compassions fail not. They are new every morning; Great is His faithfulness" (Lamentations 3:22-23).

   Beloved, the above scriptural passage should be ruminated upon, in order for you to give a down-to-heart and acceptable thanksgiving to God.
4. Thank God for His all-sufficiency in your life. You can make use of the content in Psalms 103:1-end as well as in Exodus 15:1-13 verbatim to thank the Lord. In addition, appreciate Him for all His blessings upon your life that you have physically seen and those that are yet to physically materialise.

Giving thanks simply involves counting your blessings, one by one and in turn, express your gratitude unto God for them, because:

> ***Every good gift and every perfect gift is from above, and cometh down from the Father of lights; with whom is no variableness, neither shadow of turning.*** [James 1:17]

Note: The implication of giving thanks to God is that you acknowledge Him – the Almighty, as your source and thus declaring it to Him on one hand and to the Devil and his cohorts on the other hand. By this act, you will attract more of God's favourable disposition, lifting, triumph, etc. toward your person.

Beloved, when you give thanks to God, He will make your tank to become full. Giving gratitude to God will place you on a grand stand. It takes actual thoughtfulness in a person to be able to give a whole-hearted thanksgiving to the Most High God, because, it is when a man or a woman is thoughtful that he or she can be thankful. A person who fails to give gratitude to God shall be grounded. My prayer to you, dear reader is that you shall not be grounded in the Mighty name of Jesus Christ (Amen).

Nonethless, giving thanks to God is the spiritual key that enables you to walk your way through the gates of the Almighty without hitch.Thanksgiving indeed gives you access through the gates of Jehovah El-Shaddai.

CHAPTER TWO

Praise

Another requirement to gaining entrance to the courts of the Most High God is praise. While thanksgiving takes you to His gate, praise takes you to His court. Let the following scriptural assertions be your thoughtful confession, expression and lifestyle:

> ***"It is a good thing to give thanks unto the LORD, and to sing praise unto thy name, O Most High"*** (Psalm 92:1).
>
> ***"Sing of the Mercies of the Lord forever. With your mouth make known His faithfulness"*** (Psalm 89:1).
>
> ***"Praise the Lord! Sing to the Lord a new song, praise Him in the assembly of His saints"*** (Psalm 149:1).
>
> ***"Praise the Lord! For it is good to sing praises to our God for He is gracious and lovely, praise is becoming and appropriate"*** (Psalm 147:1, Amplified Bible).

New King James Version of the Bible puts the passage of Psalm, Chapter 147 and verse 1 thus:

> ***"PRAISE the LORD! For it is good to sing praises to our God; For it is pleasant and praise is beautiful".***

The New Scofield Reference Bible puts the same passage succinctly as follows:

> ***"PRAISE ye the LORD for it is good to sing praises unto our God; for it is pleasant; and praise is fitting".***

Beloved, praising God is becoming, appropriate, pleasant, beautiful and fitting. Glory! Halleluyah!!

When you praise God, He is forced to be bodily present or make Himself available because: God inhabits the praises of His people. Also, when you praise God, the following happens:

1. God executes vengeance upon the wicked nations and peoples – Psalm 149:6-7.
2. Kings of the host of wicked are bound with chains – Psalm 149:8a.
3. The nobles of the host of wicked shall be bound with fetters of iron – Psalm 149:8b.
4. God shall execute judgment of damnation, disgrace, confusion, shame and destruction upon the wicked on your behalf.

Take note: This honour is ascribed to every son or daughter of God, who gives High praises to God with his or her mouth – Psalm 149:6,9.

Beloved, praise God! Praise Him anyhow; be it with songs, string instruments, organs, tambourine, drums, cymbal and what have you. Sing High praises to the Most High God. But, you must do it wholeheartedly.

Take further note: As you sincerely thank God and give High Praises to Him, you will experience an aura of His Splendor and presence. Holy Spirit will be present, the power and glory of God shall be evident. Ability and unction to supplicate, intercede and pray all types of answerable prayer shall become your portion. This will go a long way to make prayer an easy task for you, because:

> ***"the Spirit also helpeth our infirmity; for we know not what we should pray for as we ought; but the***

spirit himself maketh intercession for us with groaning which cannot be uttered" (Romans 8:26, Scofield Bible).

Above it, wonders, blessings and protection of God shall be our portion, as we praise the Most High God.

Let the people praise thee, O God; let all the people praise thee. Then shall the earth yield her increase; and God, even our own God shall bless us. God shall bless us; and all the ends of the earth shall fear him (Psalm 67:5-7).

CHAPTER THREE

Prayers for Deliverance and Help

1. Make haste O God to deliver me; make haste to help me oh Lord - Psalm 70: 1.
2. Let them be ashamed and confounded that seek after me and demand for my life - Psalm 70:2a.
3. Let them be turned backward and put to confusion and dishonor that desire my hurt - Psalm 70:2b.
4. Let them be turned back for a reward of their shame that say Aha, Aha! - Psalm 70:3.
5. I am poor and needy, make haste unto me, O God. You are my help and my deliverer; O LORD, make no tarrying.
6. In you, O LORD, do I put my trust and confidently make refuge; let me never be put to shame or confusion! - Psalm 71: 1.
7. Deliver me in your Righteousness and cause us (me) to escape. Bow down your ear to me and save me! - Psalm 71:2.
8. Rescue me, O my God, out of the hand of the wicked, out of the grasp of the unrighteous and ruthless man.
9. O God, be not far from me: O my God, make haste for my help - Psalm 71:12.
10. Let them be put to shame and consume them who are adversaries to my life. (Appropriate this prayer point to your family, children and loved ones.) - Psalm 71:13a.

11. Let them be covered with reproach, scorn and dishonour who seek and require our hurt – Psalm 71:13b. You can personalize this prayer point and vehemently pray it to your favour.
12. Oh Lord! God, cause my enemies to turn back, to stumble and perish before you, in Jesus' mighty name – Psalm 9:3, Amplified Bible.
13. Oh my God, rebuke all that constitute evil nations, peoples, groups and organization against my life and destiny – Psalm 9:5a.
14. Oh Most High God, cause destruction to the wicked on my behalf, on behalf of my ministry, career, family, endeavours and destiny – Psalm 9:5b.
15. Blot out the names of my enemies and those who hate me forever and ever – Psalm 9:5c.
16. Oh God, cut off my enemies and make them to vanish in everlasting ruins – Psalm 9:6a.
17. Pluck up and overthrow their cities, congregation, meeting points, homes, etc. and cause their very memory to perish and vanish – Psalm 9:6.
18. Oh God Almighty, avenge me of all my enemies and all those who gather themselves together against me unjustly – Psalm 9:12.
19. Cause the wicked nations, communities, groups, peoples, persons and or person who are against my life and destiny to sink down in the pit that they have made, are making and want to make in the name of Jesus Christ – Psalm 9:15a.
20. My father and my God, cause their feet to be caught in the net which they hid for me – Psalm 9:15a.

21. Oh my God, the Man of war, make yourself known on my behalf in the faces of my challenges, battles of life, my foes and haters of my life and destiny - Psalm 9:16a.

22. My heavenly father and the only source of my victory, execute your judgment of indignation and wrath against all the enemies and haters of my life, known and unknown, be it in the spirit or in the physical, in the victorious name of Jesus Christ - Psalm 9:16b.

23. God, arise in my favour against all my foes, wicked gathering against me and my haters, by causing them to be snared in the works of their hands - Psalm 9:16c.

24. Oh God, in your fiery anger, cause the wicked to be turned back headlong, into premature death and ultimately into sheol (the place of departed spirits of the wicked) in the triumphant name of Jesus Christ - Psalm 9:17, Amp. Bible.

25. Arise, O Lord! Let not man prevail against me, my wife, my children, loved ones, God's heritage in my charge, my destiny, etc. in Jesus name - Psalm 9:19. You can mention names of person(s), group, people, etc. that God might have revealed to you as your enemies, by His spirit one after the other, and to violently exercise yourself with this prayer point for God's intervention over them - Psalm 9:19a.

26. Oh Lord! Arise and let all the nations of wickedness, the shepherds and their flocks, men and women, male and female, young and old, the chariots and the riders be judged before you; and justify me over them, in Jesus name - Psalm 9:19.

27. Oh God, put all the foes, fowlers, enemies and haters of my life, family, careers, ministries, endeavours and destiny in fear and make them to realize their frail nature, that they may submit themselves unto you, for my safety and triumph over them all – Psm. 9:20.

28. Oh God, let the wicked who in their pride and arrogance, hotly pursue and persecute me and mine be taken in the schemes which they have devised, in Jesus' name – Psm. 10:2.

    Note: Pray this prayer point with fervency and in consonance with revelation of foes and haters of your life which God has shown to you.

29. Oh God, break the arm of the wicked and all the evil men on my behalf and search out their wickedness, until you find them no more, in Jesus' name – Psm 10:15, Amplified Bible.

30. Arise, Oh Lord! O God, lift up your hand against the foes and adversaries of my life, their thinking, imagination, deliberation, ratification and operations, in Jesus' mighty name – Psm 10:21, 11.

31. Oh God of heaven, give us great and complete deliverance from the hands and power of the enemies and from the hands of those that hate us – Psm. 18:50.

32. Almighty God, cause those who seek and demand my life to ruin and destroy it, to be destroyed and go into the lower parts of the earth (into the underworld of the dead – Psalm 63:9.

33. Father, Lord! Cause them to fall by the sword – Psalm 63:10.

34. Oh God, cause them to be a portion and prey for foxes and jackals - Psalm 63:10.

35. Oh God, my father and deliverer, shoot an unexpected arrows that would suddenly wound the wicked who make secret counsel and conspiracy of the ungodly against me, in Jesus' Mighty name - Psm. 64:2.

36. God, cause this set of people and others who whet their tongue like a sword, and aim venomous words like arrows against me to stumble - Psm. 64:8a.

37. Also, cause their own evil tongues to fall upon themselves, so much that all that see them shall shake the head and flee away - Psm. 64:8bc.

38. Oh My God, by fearful and glorious things that terrify the wicked, but make the godly sing praises, favour me and my cause on every side in the name of Jesus - Psm. 65:5.

39. Oh God! My deliverer, still the roaring of the seas of wickedness in my life Psm. 65:7a.

40. Oh Most High God, still the roaring of the waves of the Devil and all his cohorts in my life and destiny, in the name of Jesus Christ - Psm. 65:7b.

41. Oh God, the man of war, put an end to all evil tumults in my life, ministries, careers, endeavours and destiny in Jesus name - Psm 65:7,

42. My Father and my God, manifest the greatness of your power for all the enemies of my life to forcefully submit themselves unto you - Psm. 66:3b.

43. Oh my God, do the terrific and terrible act of yours in my favour and against all my foes and those who hate me - Psm. 65:5.

*Please note:*Pray this Number 43 prayer point on behalf of your spouse, children, loved ones, career, community, town, state, nation and the entire body of Christ – Psm. 66:3a.

44. Oh God! Rule in the affairs of my life and prevail against all the wicked ones that are out against my life and destiny – Psm 66:7.

45. God! Arise, and let all your enemies and the enemies of my life and destiny be scattered – Psm. 68: 1a.

46. Father God, arise and let them that hate you and hate me flee before you – Psm 68:1b.

47. As smoke is driven away, so drive them away – Psm 68:2a.

48. As wax melts before the fire, so let the wicked and those who are against me, my family and destiny perish at your presence, Oh Most High God – Psm. 68:2b.

49. God, cause the earth to shake against all my foes, fowlers and haters of my life and cause your instruments of wrath and destruction from the heavens to drop upon them for disaster – Psm 68:8.

50. Oh God of heaven, beat down all my foes before my face in accordance with your word – Psm. 89:23a.

51. Oh God! arise and plague all of them that hate me – Psm 89:23b. Pray this point for your loved ones also.

CHAPTER FOUR

Prayers of Vengeance and Recompensation of Tribulation Against Your Troublelers

"Seeing, it is a righteous thing with God to recompense tribulation to them that trouble you" (2 Thess 1:6, KJV).

The Amplified Bible puts the above scriptural passage thus:

"(It is a fair decision) since it is a righteous thing with God to repay with distress and affliction those who distress and afflict you."

God said through His prophet, Nahum, thus:

"The LORD is slow to anger and great in power, and will not at all acquit the wicked; The LORD hath his way in the whirlwind and in the storm, and the clouds are the dust of his feet."
(Nahum 1:3)

Nonetheless, it is writen that *"The LORD is good, a strong hold in the day of trouble, and he knoweth them that trust in him. But with an overrunning flood he will make an utter end of the place thereof, and darkness shall pursue the enemies"* (Nahum 1:7, 8).

Also, it is written:

"Dearly beloved, avenge not yourselves, but rather, give place unto wrath, for . . . Vengeance is mine; I will repay (requite) saith the Lord" (Romans 12:19).

PRAYER POINTS

1. Oh God arise in your righteous favour towards me, my spouse and my children to recompense with distress those who distress (me) us – 2 Thess. 1:6a.
2. Mighty God, recompense with affliction those who afflict (me) us – 2 Thess. 1:6b.
3. Mighty God, recompense failure to those who want me to be a failure and let it be impossible for me to be a failure.
4. God, trouble them who trouble me and let trouble cease in my life, affairs, endeavours and destiny.
5. Oh God, deal out retribution – chastisement and vengeance upon the wicked and infidel who surround me about and are against me, my family and destiny – 2 Thess. 1:8.
6. Father God, locate all those who are against me and your God-given purpose for my life and my family in their varied locations and deal brutally with them with retribution of disaster, destruction, shame, reproach and impoverishment.
7. God of glory, chastise and let your vengeance of wrath be upon those who are competing with and waging war against my blessings and well-being in the land of the living, in Jesus' name.
8. Oh God of vengeance, let your vengeance of tribulation, affliction, demotion, reproach, death and eternal damnation be upon every man, every woman, every young, every old, every male and female, every congregation, community, peoples etc. in their different locations who are all out against me and my family's

lives, fulfillment and destiny in Jesus' mighty name (Amen) - Nahum 1:3.

9. Arise, Oh God, and make all those who are gathered against me, against my wife, husband, children, blessings, fulfillment and destiny, etc. to fall for our sake - Isaiah 54:15.

10. Oh God of vengeance, terrorise those who terrorise me, be they in my father's house, mother's house, in-law's house, among neighbours where I live, among colleagues, among known and unknown people and let their devastation have no end or remedy in Jesus' mighty name - Isaiah 54:14b.

11. Oh God of vengeance, oppress all my oppressors and those who are out against my life for oppression - Isaiah 54:14a.

12. I condemn every tongue of men, women, male, female, young, old, shepherd, flock, witches, wizards, devils, principalities, powers, ruler of the darkness of this world and spiritual wickedness in high places risen against me with judgment of wind of destructive fire from the presence of God, in Jesus' name - Jer. 51:1.

13. I decree destruction to every detractor of my glory, fulfillment, honour, dignity, success who is against me to see that his/her evil desires come to pass in my life.

    Note: Mention names, places, peoples that God must have opened your eyes to see, while in this prayer mood.

14. Oh God! I must not die the death of men, of witches, of wizards of occults, of hazards, of the powers of darkness. Rather I shall live my life fulfilled, while I

shall see the destruction of all the wicked that surround me about, in the name of Jesus Christ (Amen).

15. Father God, defend me, my family and loved ones and crush all our oppressors and those who desire us for evil.
16. Oh God of vengeance, manifest your daily indigna-tion against and upon those who are indignant to me in the name of Jesus' Christ - Psm 7:11.
17. Oh God of vengeance, cause your whet sword to pierce the bosom of the wicked, who have refused to repent and desist from doing wickedness to me, my home, my work, my ministries, my destiny and my fulfillment in life and through eternity in Jesus name - Psm. 7:12a.
18. Oh God, my father, in your vengeance spare not, but make use of your deadly weapons to wreck havoc and massacre to the lives and camps of my enemies and haters of my life - Psm. 7:13a.
19. Oh God, the man of war, cause your arrows fiery shafts to be shut and pierce into the hearts and beings of my adversaries in their legions and locations in Jesus' name.
20. And let it be impossible for anyone among my enemies and haters to escape the destructive effects of your arrows upon their lives.
21. Oh God, let and push the wicked to fall into his (their) evil conception that he or they conceive against me and my family, in Jesus' name - Psm 7:14a.
22. Oh God of vengeance, let the wicked die and be doomed eternally by the pregnancy of mischief which they are impregnated with against me, my household and my blessings, in Jesus' mighty name - Ps. 7:14b.

23. Oh God of vengeance, cause the wicked man, the wicked woman, the wicked female, the wicked male (you can mention names as God might have revealed to you) to be enmeshed in the destruction of his/her lies which he/she gives birth to against me and all mine, in Jesus' name - Psm 7:14c.

24. Oh God of vengeance, cause and push the wicked who are assigned against my life to fall into and be buried in the pit which they have made and hollowed out in Jesus name - Psm 7:15.

25. Father God of vengeance, cause the wicked and dragons of darkness assigned against my life and destiny to have their mischief fall back in return upon their own head and upon the heads of every member of their household - Psm 7:16a.

26. Oh God of vengeance, cause violence of the wicked and evil people assigned against my life and destiny to come down upon their scalp - Psm. 7:16b.

27. Oh God, in your vengeance on my behalf, raise wind of destruction against the wicked that constitute obstacles to the wheel of progress of my life in the name of Jesus Christ - Jer. 51:1; Nahum 1:7-8.

28. God of vengeance, raise destroying wind against those who constitute themselves as Babylon to my life and destiny; and those who stand with them, in Jesus' name - Jer. 51:1.

29. Oh God, to whom vengeance belongs, show yourself on my behalf by frustrating the tokens of liars, who are against me, my family, my God-given assignments and my destiny, in Jesus' name - Isaiah 44:25a.

30. Oh my God, avenge me of all my enemies and haters by making all diviners against my life, family, missions on earth, endeavours and destiny to be made mad – Isaiah 44:25b.

31. Oh God, in your vengeance, turn all those who prove wise against my total well-being backward and make their knowledge foolish – Isaiah 44:25c.

32. Oh God, in your vengeance, cause everyone who has dug pit for me, to fall therein and let it be impossible for me and any of my family members and loved ones to fall into the pit, in Jesus' mighty name – Proverbs 26:27a.

33. Oh Lord, my father, in your vengeance on my behalf, cause stones rolled to me and my loved ones by the wicked to return upon him/her (them) –Proverb 26:27b.

34. Oh God of vengeance, cause affliction to everyone, who out of hatred makes use of lying tongues against me, in the name of Jesus Christ – Prov. 26:28a.

    Note: You can mention names, as revealed to you by the Holy Spirit while violently praying this prayer point.

35. Oh God of vengeance, ruin every person, people, peoples and evil gathering who are out to use their flattering mouths to work out my ruin – Proverbs 26:28b.

36. Oh God of vengeance, be a terror unto all that hate me and are out to terrorise me, in the name of Jesus Christ – Jer. 17:17a.

37. Father God, in your vengeance, cause evil to befall all those that are risen against me, but be my hope continuously in the day of evil, in Jesus name – Jer. 7:17b.

38. Oh God, in your vengeance, on my behalf, let them be confounded that persecute me, but let me not be confounded – Jeremiah 17:18a.
39. Oh God, in your vengeance, let them be dismayed that persecute me – Jer. 17:18b.
40. Oh my God, in your fight for me, bring upon them the day of evil, all that persecute me and are against my life, in Jesus name – Jer. 17:18c.
41. Mighty God in battle, arise in your vengeance on my behalf and destroy all them that persecute me with double destruction, in the name of Jesus Christ – Jer. 17:18d.
42. Oh God, my warrior in battle, let your irrevocable curses be unleashed upon those who are gathered negatively against me and my God-given projects and mission on earth, in the name of Jesus Christ – Jer. 17:5a.
43. Let them all be like the heat in the desert – Jer. 17:6a.
44. Let them never see good all the days of their lives – Jer. 17:6b.
45. Let them inhabit the parched places in the wilder-ness – Jer. 17:6c.
46. Cause their habitation not to be habitable and in a salt land – Jer. 17:6d.
47. Let fruitfulness be far away from them on every side and in all their endeavours – Jer. 17:6.
48. Let unfruitness and barrenness be their total portion in every issue of their lives, in the name of Jesus.
49. Cause them to be written in the earth because they are against me, whom you have chosen, my LORD and the fountain of living waters – Jer. 17:13.

50. Oh my God, in your favour towards me (us) and in your vengeance against my (our) foes, fowlers, and haters of my (our) life(ves) and destiny, prove yourself on my (our) behalf and prevail against them all, for my (our) victory to be established.

CHAPTER FIVE

Victorious Prayers for Fortification, Stability and Establishment

> *In righteousness shall you be established, you shall be far from oppression; for you shall not fear; and from terror, for it shall not come near you"* (Isaiah 54:14).

The Lord God also said:

> *"Behold, they shall surely gather together but not by me: whosoever shall gather together against you shall fall for your sake"*(Isaiah 54:15).

Nevertheless, the Lord said unequivocally the following words of re-assurance for your victorious establishment:

> *". . . the mountains shall depart and the hills be removed, but my kindness shall not depart from thee, neither shall the covenant of my peace be removed saith the LORD that hath mercy on thee"* (Isaiah 54:10).

PRAYER POINTS

1. Unto, you, LORD, do I lift up my soul, O my God, I trust in you: let me not be ashamed, let not my enemies triumph over me - Psm 25:1, 2.

   Note: This above prayer point is a song and prayer. Endeavour to register it on your heart, sing the song and pray it fervently always for your triumphant establishment, fortification and stability.

2. Oh God of heaven, I receive sufficient grace from you to maintain righteous lifestyle and to be an epitome of righteousness, in Jesus, name – Rom. 14:17a; Isaiah 54:14.
3. Father God, establish me in the righteousness of your kingdom in my sojourning on this planet earth, in Jesus' mighty name – Isaiah 54:14.
4. Oh God of heaven, saturate my life with three expressive components of the kingdom, that is: righteousness, peace and joy in the Holy Ghost; and establish me in the same – Rom. 14 :17.
5. Oh my God, let it be impossible for me to be a victim of oppression, and let everything that is called oppression be far from me, in Jesus' name (Amen) – Isaiah 54: 14a.
6. Oh my God, empower and establish me to be far from terror and for terror not to come near me – Isiah 54:14b.
7. Oh God, establish me in peace and tranquility by stopping the noise of the seas, the noise of their waves, and the tumult of strange and wicked people round about me in the name of Jesus Christ – Psm 65:7.
8. Oh my God who by your strength you set fast the mountains being girded with power, be an impenetrable mountain that is girded with power around me, around my spouse, around my children and around my God-given projects in the land of the living – Psm 65:6.
9. Oh my God, establish me with the greatness of your power, so much that all my enemies and your enemies shall submit themselves unto me and unto you, in the name of Jesus Christ – Psm 66:3b.

10. Oh mighty God, rule mightily by your power, in and through me, all the days of my life in such an awesome way that will never give room for the rebellious, the ungodly and the wicked to exalt themselves, in Jesus' might name - Psm 66:7.
11. Oh God Almighty, increase my greatness and comfort me on every side, in accordance with your word - Psm 71:21.
12. Oh Great God, engrace and empower me so much that I will walk, move, live and do everything in your strength, all the days of my life - Psm 71:16.
13. Oh Most High God, engrace and help me to put my absolute trust in you - Psm 71:1a.
14. Oh my God, let me never be put to confusion, all the days of my life - Psm 71:1b.
15. Oh God of heaven and earth, be thou my strong habitation, where unto I may continually resort - Psm 71:3a.
16. Father God, help me to continually hold unto you as my rock and fortress for ever and ever, in Jesus' name - Psm 71:3b.
17. Oh God, be my daily deliverer out of the hands of the wicked, the unrighteous and cruel man or people, in Jesus' mighty name - Psm 71:4.
18. Oh God of heaven, be thou my ever strong refuge and let my mouth be filled with your praise and honour all the days of my life - Psm 71:7.
19. Oh my God, let it be impossible for you to cast me off at any time of my life, be it in the time of old age or when my strength fails - Psm 71:9.

20. Oh my God, continuously guide me with your counsel and let my end be such that you shall receive me to glory – Psm 72:24.

21. Oh God, permanently silence the enemies who are roaring against me, my family and your congrega-tion in my care, and burn off their banners for which they set up for signs, in the name of Jesus Christ – Psalm 74:4.

22. Oh God, be a shield of vengeance of eternal fire in my favour and against my foes and those who hate me – Psm 46:1; Jude 7.

23. Oh God, my refuge and strength, be a pillar of fire round about me, before me and a thick cloud behind me for my sure protection and for me to become unaccessible and unreachable to my enemies – Psm 46:1; Exod. 13:21; Neh. 9:12.

24. Oh my God, position yourself as a consuming fire in my favour and against the wicked who surround me about, all the days of my life, in Jesus name – Heb. 12:29.

25. Oh my Lord, let fire from you readily come upon and consume every person, every force, every congregation and every people and peoples who are against me, my mission on earth and destiny in the name of Jesus Christ – Lev. 10:2.

26. Oh my God, by fire and sword, execute judgment upon every foe and the wicked that are risen and gathered against me, and let the slain that you make of them be many, in Jesus mighty name – Isaiah 66:16.

27. Oh my God, in your favour to me, verily come in fire and in your chariots that are like the stormy wind to render your anger with your fierceness on (your) my foes and those who gather and operate rebuke with

flame of fire against my fulfillment and the fulfillment of my posterity, in Jesus' mighty name - Isaiah 66:15, Amplified Bible.

28. Oh my God, in your mercy, deliver me from blood guiltiness and justify me by the blood of covenant of the Lord Jesus Christ that was shed for remission of my sin and redemption of mankind - Psm 51:14; Heb. 9:22; 10:29; 13:20; Eph 1:7; Col. 1:14; Rom. 5:9.

29. Oh God, justify me by the blood of Jesus and condemn my foes, fowlers and haters of my life by the efficacy of the blood - Rom. 5:9.

30. Oh God, cover and establish me and all my God-given assignments and project on earth by the covering of the blood of Jesus Christ - Exod. 12:13.

31. By the blood of everlasting covenant, I decree the establishment of impregnable stronghold against evil incursion all around me, my family, my endeavours, commission and facilities of the commission - Zech. 9:12.

32. By the blood of Jesus Christ, I receive defence to me, my family, commission and the body of Christ in Nigeria and worldwide by devouring and subduing everyone that is against our peace and safety and the peace and safety of the elect - Zech. 9:15.

33. Father-God, by the efficacy of the blood of Jesus Christ, release your arrow of death like the lightening into the camp of all the enemies of God, harassing, insulring and assaulting me, my family, my commission and the body of Christ at large - Zech. 9:14.

34. Father, by the blood of Jesus Christ, cut off from the earth, all perpetrators, sympathizers and sponsors of

those who are shedding the blood of saints and particularly those who are against me and my family far and near in the name of Jesus Christ - Zech. 9:16.

35. God, make your word be as fire in my bones to burn off every strange deposits, and planting in my life and for me to become an untouchable fire to the devil, his cohorts and host of wickedness, in the name of Jesus' Christ - Jer. 20:9.

36. Oh God, let your peace dominate me and all that are mine and let it be the hallmark within my wall and surroundings, in Jesus' might name - Psalm 122:7.

37. Oh God, by your power, and by the power in the blood, let it be that violence shall no more be heard in my land, in my house, in my facilities, in my commission and in my domain, in Jesus' might name - Isaiah 60:18a.

38. Oh my God, by your almightiness, let it be that neither wasting nor destruction shall be heard within my borders, in Jesus name - Isaiah 60:18b.

39. Oh my God, by your word and power, let it be that my walls shall be called salvation and my gates praise by me and by all and sundry in Jesus' mighty name - Isaiah 60:18c.

40. My Father and my God, anoint me with great and fresh anointing that will make it impossible for the enemy to exact upon me or do me violence or outwit me - Psalm 89:22a.

41. Oh God, greatly and mightily anoint me afresh so that with me, your hand shall be established and ever abide and your arm shall strengthen me - Psm 89:21 Amp. Bible.

42. Oh my Father God, by your mighty hand upon me and your strength in me, let it be that it shall be impossible for the wicked to afflict and humble me - Psm 89:22b.

43. Father God, let your hand be mighty upon me and ever abiding and let your arm strengthen me so much that you will ceaselessly beat down my foes before my face and smite those who hate me - Psm 89:23.

44. Oh my God, by your anointing upon me and within me, set my hand in control over all things in heaven, on earth, under the earth, in the sea, on the sea, in the air and in all situations, in Jesus' mighty name - Psm 89:25.

45. Oh God, establish me with your mighty hands upon me so much that my cry to you shall ceaselessly be that you are my father, my God and the rock of my salvation - Psm 89:26.

46. Oh my God, according to your promise, keep your mercy and loving-kindness for me forever and let your covenant stand fast and be faithful with me, in Jesus' name - Psm 89:28.

47. Oh my God, make my offspring to endure forever - Psm. 89:29, 36.

48. Father God, by your covenant, do not ever forsake me and my children at anytime and for any reason. Even at the point of breaking or forsaking your law, correct us and enforce our turning unto you, through eternity, in Jesus' name - Psm 89:30-33.

49. Oh God, establish the throne in which you have enthroned me as the sun before you forever and as the moon, in Jesus' name - Psm 89:36-37.

50. Make me and my offsprings radiants of your glory forever and let anyone who curses us be cursed: and

anyone who blesses us to be blessed; and whosoever we curse to be cursed, and whosoever we bless, to be blessed.

51. Also, in blessing, bless me and multiply my seed as the stars of the heaven and as the sand upon the seashore and cause my seeds to possess the gates of their enemies and through them shall the nation of the earth be blessed – Gen. 12:3; 22:17, 18; 2 Chr. 7:1.

CHAPTER SIX

Dangerous Triumphant Decree/ Declarative Prayers

> *"Thus saith the Lord, thy redeemer, and he who formed thee from the womb: I am the Lord who maketh all things, who stretcheth forth the heavens alone, who spreads abroad the earth by myself. Who frustrates the signs of the babbler and drive diviners mad. Who turns wise men backward and makes their knowledge become foolishness. Who confirms the word of his servant and performs the counsel of his messengers"* (Isaiah 44:24-26).

It is written in Job, chapter 22 and verse 28 that:

> *"Thou shall also decree a thing, and it shall be established unto thee and the light shall shine upon thy ways"* (Scofield Reference Bible).

The above scriptural passage is put by Samuel O. Jimson's version of the Bible thus: *"You shall also decide, decree and declare a thing, and it shall be established for you, and the light (of God's favour and presence) shall shine upon your ways because the God of our salvation who is the confidence and hope of all the ends of the earth and of those that are far off on the seas answers our prayers unto Him in righteousness, by terrible, fearful, glorious and awesome things (that terrify the wicked, but make the godly sing praise)"* - Psm. 65:5.

PRAYERS

1. I decree and declare the storm of fire from the Lord to fall into the camps of my enemies and the enemies of

God in their different locations to cause disaster, disarray, upheaval and catastrophe to them and to their evil instrument, In Jesus' mighty name.

3. I declare and decree a destroying wind from the LORD to be risen against those who constitute themselves as Babylon in my life, in my household and in my destiny and against those who dwell among them, in one way or the other, and those who have affinity with them – Jer. 51:1.

4. I decree winnowers from the Lord to winnow and empty the land of all that constitute themselves as Babylon in my life and destiny in Jesus' name – Jer. 51:2a.

4. Oh God, I decree winnowers from you to arise against every man, every woman, every male, every female, every young, every old, every group, every people, those near and those far away who constitute themselves as Babylon to my life, household and destiny on every side in the day of calamity in Jesus' name – Jer. 51:2b.

5. I decree the archer to bend his bow against them in Jesus' name – Jer 51:3a.

6. I decree the archer to lift himself up against them in their armor and to my favour in Jesus' name – Jer. 51:3b.

7. I decree and declare that their young men shall not be spared and all their army shall be utterly destroyed, in the name of Jesus Christ – Jer. 51:3c.

8. According to the word of the Lord, I decree and declare slain to fall in the hand, gathering, street, and camp of the wicked, my enemies and the enemies of God's will

and mandate for my life, in Jesus mighty name - Jer. 51:4a.

9. I declare and decree the same nemesis of being slain to fall upon home and street of every one who is friendly, related, in connivance and conspiracy with them who constitute themselves as Babylon, enemies and haters to me, my household and our destinies in Jesus name - Jer. 51:4b.

10. I decree the vengeance of the Lord, to recompense to everyone who represents Babylon to my life, my household, my God-given mandate on earth and my destiny, in Jesus mighty name - Jer. 51:6.

11. I command, decree and declare sudden irreparable fallen and destruction to all that constitute themselves as Babylon and their installation against my life, my household and destiny in the name of Jesus Christ - Jer. 51:8.

12. Oh God, I decree in your vengeance that utter destruction should come upon every enemy and hater of my life for all his or her evil against me - your anointed and your Prophet - Jer 51:11.

13. I decree and declare God's standard to be set upon the walls of all that constitute Babylon against my life, household and destiny and prepare ambushment against them and all those who are with them for their utter destruction - Jer 51:12.

14. Oh force of darkness and enemies of my well-being and total freedom and fulfillment of my destiny who operate upon many waters and in abundance of your treasure, I decree and declare your end and destruction in and over my life and destiny, in Jesus' name - Jer. 51:13.

15. I decree God to fill you the host of wicked and those that constitute Babylon against my life with men, as with caterpillars, who shall lift up a shout against you for your shame and destruction, in the name of Jesus Christ – Jer. 51:14.
16. I decree and declare God's spiritual cord missile to be sent into the camp of my accusers, assailants and those who are risen against me for their destruction, in Jesus' name.
17. I pull down and destroy every stronghold of setback, intimidation, blockades, obstacle, failure, poverty and penury set against my life and destiny by the power and fire of the Holy Spirit, by the power in the blood of Jesus, by the word of God which is like fire that burns and like hammer that breaks the rock into pieces, in the name of Jesus Christ.
18. By the efficacy of the name of Jesus, by the power and fire of the Holy Spirit and by the efficacy of the word of God that is like hammer that breaks the rock into pieces, I command destruction to the network installation and operations of the devil and his cohorts against my life, works, careers, efforts made for progress, endeavours, ministry, family, and I decree utter destruction to their power and influence upon all that concern me in the name of Jesus Christ.
19. You Devil, principalities and power, rulers of the darkness of this world, spiritual wickedness in high places, witches, wizards, Ogbonis, Osugbo, Gbarayile, Alawopa, Onitabatiada, Oni Ontu, and forces of darkness, operating in the seas, on the sea, under the sea, in the water, under the waters, on the water; on the rock and under the rock; on the tree, in the tree, in the

air, in the atmosphere and under, in levels 333, to 999, I decree by the blood of Jesus Christ, by the power and fire of the Holy Spirit and by the efficacy of the word of God that you stop in all your operations against my life, total well being and my fulfillment, right from my mother's womb, what you have been doing since I have been born into this world, what you are doing currently and what you are yet to do and desist in your manouver concerning every facet of my life, in Jesus' mighty name.

20. I decree that all you people that are associated together against me, be broken into pieces, be it from the neighborhood of my residence; neighbour-hood of where I work, be it from enemies, foes, detractors and haters of my life and destiny at any location, be broken into pieces in the name of Jesus Christ - Isaiah 8:9a.

21. All you that make an uproar or associate yourself to make an uproar against me, my house hold and my blessings, I decree and declare that ye be broken into pieces and shall/should be broken into pieces in the name of Jesus Christ - Isiah 8:9a, Ampl. Bible.

22. O you people-raging, raising the war cry against me, my household, my destiny and my fulfillment, I declare and decree that you should be utterly dismayed and be broken into pieces - Isaiah 9b.

23. Give ear all you our enemies of far countries; gird your selves for war, be thrown into consternation and broken into pieces; gird your selves and ye shall be utterly dismayed and be broken into pieces, in the mighty name of Jesus Christ - Isaiah 8:9bc.

24. I decree nullity to all your counsel against me, my present and future, your counsel against my household's present and future and your counsel against my success, in the mighty name of Jesus – Isaiah 8:10a.

25. I decree that none of the words that you have spoken or that you shall speak against me on any issue or facet of my life and that of my family members and destiny shall stand, because God is with us, in the name of Jesus Christ – Isaiah 8:10b.

26. I decree and declare that the Most High God should be for a stone of stumbling and for a rock of offence, for a trap and for a snare for your stumbling, falling, for you to be broken, snared and taken, oh you people, far and near, known and unknown and you forces of wickedness that are out against me, my family, our destinies and fulfillment in the mighty name of Jesus Christ – Isaiah 8:14, 15.

    Note that names of people and forces in their different locations should be mentioned while praying this prayer point.

27. I decree nullity to the confederacy of my enemies and haters of my life and destiny, wherever you are and I declare God's fire of destruction upon your heads for your utter destruction in the mighty name of Jesus Christ – Isaiah 8:12.

28. As God's battle axe and His weapon of war, I break into pieces all nations of witches, wizards, familiar spirit, marine spiritual world and occult that are against God's will and work in my life and those of my family

members; and through us in the powerful name of Jesus Christ - Jer. 51:20a.

29. As God's battle axe and His weapon of war, I break into pieces all nations of conspirators and evil operators against God's will, God's operation, counsel and mission for my life and destiny, in the name of Jesus Christ - Isaiah 51:20a.

30. As God's battle axe and his weapon of war, I break into pieces the kings, queens, princes and princesses of the regions of darkness and their followers that are positioned against my life and the lives of my family members and those who are loyal to God's will concerning my life, in the name of Jesus Christ - Jer. 51:20a.

31. As God's battle axe and His weapon of war, I destroy the kingdoms of Muslim, Jihadists, witches, ogbonis, wizards, familiar spirit, mammy water's spirits, ogbanje spirit, osugbos spirits, alawopas spirit, herbalist, voodooist, spiritualists and all agent of darkness who are against my life, my family, my God-given mission, destiny, in my environment in Oyo State (mention the state you are) in Nigeria, in West Africa, in African continent, in the USA, Canada, UK, etc. in the victorious name of Jesus Christ - Jer 51:20b.

32. As God's battle axe and His weapon of war, I break in pieces all that represent horses and their riders against my life and destiny and from any location, in the name of Jesus Christ - Jer. 51:21a.

33. As God's battle axe and His weapon of war, I break in pieces all you that represent chariots and your riders against my life, well-being, blessings and fulfillment in the land of the living, in Jesus' name - Jer 51:21b.

34. As God's battle axe and His weapon of war, I break in pieces, every man and woman, every old man and woman, young man and maiden operating, speaking and unleashing wickedness against me, my family, my facilities, destiny and fulfillment from my neighbourhood, the town, city, village, state, nation where I live and far and near in the mysterious name of Jesus Christ – Jer. 51:22.

    Note: You can pray, making mention of names of men women, young, old, male and female separately, that God might have revealed to you by His Spirit while praying this point as situation demands.

35. I break in pieces every shepherd and flock, in whatever name they bear and in any location of theirs, who are gathered, gathering or would want to gather, praying or using any means of wickedness against me, the works of God in and through my hands, my ministries, careers, my family, my helpers and loved ones in the mighty name of Jesus Christ – Jer. 51:23a.

    (Pray this point fervently without any sentiment for your victory).

TESTIMONIES

For no good reason known to me, a so called Pastor in the neighbourhood of where I currently reside with my family gathered six other people with him, making seven people in number, who have been living in that environment before God moved us there. The said Pastor's single mission for gathering the people was that my corpse could be brought to my new house, which was yet to be completed then. However, to God's glory, we moved into the apartment, hail and hearty and have been there for over eight years now. Halleluyah! Additionally, a storey building office/shopping complex has been put in place, directly in front of that same apartment within the short pace of time. Glory be to God in the Highest.

Also, after we newly moved to the apartment, while some landlords came to say hello to us, this same Pastor failed to come with them. However, I invited him to connect electric wire from the pole into the same building being an electrician, which he did and I paid him for his services and gave him a bottle of soft drink for his refreshment. What I noticed, while the man was doing the electrical connection from the pole into my apartment was his unhappy mood. But, he did the work. This is one of many reasons why the above number 35 prayer point should be said without reservation, but with the help of the Holy Spirit, and should be said continuously.

Read the book ***Victory In Your Zero Hour, A Compendium of God's Intervention in Your Miserable and Difficult Situations***, by this same author.

36. I decree wind of destruction from God's treasure to be unleashed upon my enemies and haters of mine and my family's well being and fulfillment, for utter destruction, in the name of Jesus Christ - Jer. 51:16c.

37. Oh God of heaven, visit all my foes, fowlers and enemies of my life, family, ministries, career, success and destiny with visitation that will make them all perish, but for our lifting, fulfillment and glory in Jesus' name - Jer. 51:18.

38. I decree mysterious lion out of forest to slay as many have chosen to be on the devil and animous side against

me, my family and my destiny through eternity, in the name of Jesus Christ - Jer. 5:6a.

39. In the mighty name of Jesus Christ, I decree mysterious wolf of the day, evening and night to devour as many as are on the devil's side against God's will, God's works, God's blessings and His glory in and upon my life and family, in the name of the Lord Jesus Christ - Jer. 5:6b.
40. I decree and declare that all that are incensed against me shall be vulnerable to the devourer and they shall be a prey to the lion of this wicked world without means of escape, in the mighty name of Jesus Christ - Jer. 5:6.
41. Oh God, my defence, as your eye watches over me and my family, and those who fear you and follow your ways, I decree mysterious leopard, that is, fierce flesh eaters to be watch over the wicked and those who are gathered and incensed against me, my family and God's mandates for our lives and destiny, in the mighty name of Jesus' Christ - Jer. 5:4, 5b, 5c, 5d.
42. All evil gatherers who are incensed against me, my family and God's counsel concerning us and our destiny, I decree that all of you should be vulnerable to large fierce flesh eaters; terror, labour and sorrow shall be your lot on daily basis in the name of Jesus Christ - Jer. 5:4, 5.
43. Oh God of vengeance, who is terrible in battle, arise and deliver all the people and evil gatherers against me, my loved ones, God-given mandates and destiny in all the kingdoms of the earth for their hurt, to be a reproach, a proverb, a taunt and a curse where you shall drive them in the mighty name of Jesus Christ - Jer. 24:9.

44. Oh God of heaven, send the sword, the famine and pestilence among men, women, male, female young and old, shepherd and flock, families and single, congregation of occults and the wicked ones, who are against me, my family and destiny, in their different locations until they are consumed from the land of the living, in the mighty name of Jesus Christ - Jer. 24:10.

45. Oh God, who fights my battles on my behalf, I decree and declare speedy punishment and your called sword to come upon all the habitation of the wicked, who are assigned and working against me, my family, my God-given visions, mandates and destiny, in the name of Jesus Christ - Jer. 25:29.

46. Oh God, in your controversy against my fowlers and those who are risen against me and against fulfillment of my destiny, roar from on high, cause a noise to come to the ends of the earth and give them all and their cohorts of wickedness to the sword, in the mighty name of Jesus Christ - Jer. 25:31.

47. I decree violence to be a common occurrence in the land, location, home, congregation and meeting point of all those who are against my life, my commission, all that concern me and my destiny. Wasting and destruction shall be within their borders; but my walls shall be called salvation and my gates praise - Isaiah 60:18.

48. I decree that all my fowlers shall grope in darkness during the day as in the night, while I invoke, declare and establish that the Lord shall be unto me and my family an everlasting light and our God and our glory, in the name of Jesus Christ - Isaiah 60:19.

49. I declare that my sun shall no more go down, neither shall my moon withdraw itself, for the Lord shall be my everlasting light and the days of my mourning shall be ended – Isaiah 60:20.

50. I decree and declare that a little one of my person and every member of my family shall become a thousand, and a small one of my person and family's one, a strong nation, which the Lord will hasten in His time – Isaiah 60:22.

CHAPTER SEVEN

Prayer Point for Prosperity and Success

1. Oh God, the giver of power for me to create and get wealthy, I pray you, to empower me with your spirit for creativity that will enhance me for wealth - Deut. 8:18.

2. I receive grace and power from the Most High God for all-encompassing prosperity for my life-spiritually, physically, financially, materially, socially and matrimonially, in the wonderful name of Jesus Christ - 3 John 2.

3. I invoke prosperity for me, my family and loved ones financially, materially, physically and in our health, above all things, in the name of Jesus Christ - 3 John 2.

4. Father, I pull down every strong hold of wicked-ness that is designed against my God-given power and creative ability to get wealth, in the name of Jesus Christ - 2 Cor. 3:2, 3; Deut. 8:18.

5. I stand my ground in Christ Jesus, against every force and power of darkness that are out against God's supreme will for my life - spiritually, physically, financially, materially, matrimonially, in Jesus mighty name.

6. God, arise against every man, every woman, every force, every power, and host of wickedness that are risen against my total prosperity and success in life, in Jesus name.

7. Oh Most High God, avail on my behalf, against every man, every woman, every male, every female, every

young and old, and gathering of wickedness that are out against my total well-being, prosperity and success; and put an end to them and their operations in my life, in Jesus' mighty name.

8. Father God, I receive grace, motivation and empowerment to make it a point of duty for book of the law not to depart from my mouth and to make it my assignment to meditate in it day and night, in Jesus mighty name - Joshua 1:8.
9. I receive grace and enablement of the spirit to observe to do according to all that is written in the word of God, so that I can make my way prosperous and have a good success - Joshua 1:8.
10. I receive grace to possess what it takes to be strong and of good courage, required of me to be prosperous and have a good success, in Jesus' name - Joshua 1:6a.
11. Oh my God, engrace and empower me enough to be bold and fearless in every situation on the path way of success for my success and prosperity to be made manifest in the mighty name of Jesus Christ - Joshua 1:6b.
12. Oh God, the source of my prosperity, empower me to be strong and courageous to observe to do according to the law of success and prosperity, in the name of Jesus Christ - Joshua 1:7.
13. Oh God! I receive your grace to be courageous and strong enough to remember and walk in the reality of your covenant for my prosperity and good success, in Jesus name - Joshua 1:5.
14. Oh my God, the man of war, empower, help me and lead me through triumphant procession unto my

destination of prosperity and success in the name of Jesus Christ - 2 Cor. 2:14.

15. Oh my God, remember your covenant and fulfill your promise to prosper me and make me to become a good success in Jesus name - 2 Cor. 1:20.

16. Oh my God, anoint and establish me in your prosperity and success in Jesus' name - 2 Cor. 1:21-22.

17. Oh my God, teach me to profit and lead me by the way that I should go in Jesus name - Isaiah 48:17.

18. Oh my God, since the way of a man is not in himself, it is not in man that walketh to direct his steps, lead and give me direction on what to do, in order to be prosperous and have a very good success, in Jesus' name - Jer. 10:23.

19. Oh my God, teach and instruct me on what to do and all that it requires of me, in order for me, to be a success with ease that emanates from you, in Jesus' name - Psm. 32:8.

20. Oh God, guard and guide me into the destination of my prosperity and success so that I will not be like the horse or the mule, which lacks understanding and which must have their mouths held firm with bit and bridle, else they will not come with you, in Jesus' name - Psm. 32:8b, 9.

21. Oh Lord God, engrace me to trust, rely on and confidently lean on you, so that I shall be compassed about with mercy and with loving kindness in my voyage to my destination of prosperity and success - Psm. 32:10, Ampl. Bible.

22. Oh God, my refuge, strength and deliverer, my times are in your hand, deliver me from the hand of my foes and those who pursue me and persecute me, as I embark on this destiny voyage in life and ministry, unto prosperity and good success – Psm. 31:15.

23. Oh God, I receive grace, power and motivation for hard work in the fields of my calling, in order for me to prosper and be a success in it – 1 Cor. 4:12; Eph. 4:28; 1 Thes. 4:11.

24. Oh God, I receive grace, wisdom and power for me to maintain a hand of the diligent, in order for me to be rich, prosperous and become a success in Jesus' name – Prov. 10:4b.

25. The all wise God, engrace and saturate me with your wisdom for me to be diligent and skillful in my business, in order for me to stand before kings and not stand before mere and obscure men – Prov. 22:29.

26. Oh my God, I receive grace to be just and upright in all my endeavours in this life voyage, so that blessings shall be upon my head – Prov. 10:6, Amp. Bible.

27. I command destruction to every yoke of unrighteousness in my life, which is capable of keeping me in penury and for my soul to famish, and I receive the spirit and power of uncom-promisingly righteous, which attracts God's favor, towards me and that will not allow me to famish – Prov. 10:3.

28. I receive grace to live righteous and embrace the garment of righteousness upon my life, which has the capability of delivering me from death, in the name of Jesus Christ – Prov. 10:2.

29. Oh God of heaven, I commit my all into your hands, let it be impossible for me to draw back from you, in truth and in spirit, even, at the height of success, in Jesus' name.

30. Father God, engrace, help and strengthen me to live in the reality that what I am and what I have, are yours, and for me to totally submit and abandon all unto you in Jesus' mighty name.

31. Oh God, enrich me so much to be able to have more than enough to meet my immediate needs, in order to be a blessing to your work, the household of faith at large and to the poor, in Jesus' name.

32. Oh God, make me relevant in your kingdom on earth and to your glory, with abundant riches, through eternity in Jesus' name.

33. Oh God, make me what I should be and all that I have to be to manifest your glory and praise, in the land of the living, in Jesus' name - 1 Pet 2:9, 10.

34. Oh God, at all times, be a great covering and shield for me, my family, loved ones and all that you have given me, for the wicked not to have access to us all, in Jesus' name.

35. Oh God, at all times, be an enemy to those who are enemies to my life, possession and blessings; and be a terror to them, who terrorise me, in Jesus' name.

36. Oh God, my defence, pressurize them all that are out against me, unto submission to you, and to their shame, but to your praise and for my blessing, in Jesus' name.

37. Oh God, as you put an end to Pharaoh and to the hosts of Egyptian army who were after the people of Israel in

the red sea, put an end to all the enemies of my prosperity and success, in Jesus' name.

38. Oh God, I let go and let you, fight on the battle on my behalf and let me see your salvation as you utterly destroy the host of wicked that are risen against me, my prosperity and success, in Jesus name [Allow the Holy Spirit to intercede for you in this direction as you pray in an unknown tongue] – Exod. 14:14; Rom. 8:26.

39. Oh God, open my eyes into your hidden treasure for my life, which will catapult me to that glorious destiny that you had earmarked for me, in the land of the living.

40. Oh God, destroy and burn down by your fire from heaven, those who represent thorn in my life and destiny, and are adverse to my speedy and hitch-free prosperity and success, in Jesus' name.

41. Oh God, I receive wisdom, understanding and knowledge, requisite to your abundant riches and blessings upon my life, in the mighty name of Jesus Christ – Prov. 24:3, 4.

42. I receive grace, never to envy sinners, but empower me to continue in the reverent and worshipful fear of the Lord, all the day long, so that my sure latter end and expectation shall not be cut off, in the name of Jesus Christ – Prov. 23:17, 18.

43. Oh God, announce my work, career, ministries and endeavours; and jealously protect all from both internal and external invasion and for my victorious prosperity and success in the name of Jesus Christ.

44. Oh God and my deliverer, utterly put to shame and destroy those who are adversaries to my careers,

ministries and the works of my hand, through my prosperity and success, in Jesus' Name.

45. Father God, establish and empower me in the headship position and status where you placed me, in Jesus' name.
46. I receive grace to develop and fully manifest all the required virtues for greatness and true success, in the name of Jesus Christ.
47. Oh my God, as you lift me up, enlarge and take me to my destination of success, cause all evil eyes to fail concerning me and spare no one who takes any adverse step or makes adverse utterances against me. Let me see their falling with my own eyes and or hear about same with my ears, in the name of Jesus Christ.
48. Oh God, endue and crown me with success and grant unto me all the required ingredients and equipments for its sustainability, for my manifesta-tions to your glory.
49. The supreme wisdom from you, backing my prosperity and progressive success, I fully receive from you, oh my God, in the name of Jesus Christ.
50. Angels of God, in charge and assigned for my prosperity and success, be on guard and in full operation to every nook and cranny of the whole world and depth of the earth and seas; and bring my blessings, prosperity and success to pass, in the mighty name of Jesus Christ.

CHAPTER EIGHT

Prayer Points for Help and Helpers

"I will lift up mine eyes unto the hills, from whence cometh my help. My help cometh from the Lord, which made heaven and earth" (Psm. 121:1, 2; 124:8).

Our help comes from the Lord God. He is the supreme Helper from whom every other helpers are sourced. In other words, while God is our major Helper and only source of help, He has person, persons, people, peoples, in all nations of the earth, that He had predestined from the foundations of the earth, to help, participate and be involved in realizing our fulfilling end. They are called Destiny helpers.

Note: The Almighty God is the only personality who can make us come in contact with and or connect us/them and work in them, both to will and bring into actualization the help, participation and action that will engender our fulfillments in life and destiny.

PRAYER PROPER

1. Oh God, my Help and Helper, raise help for me in every area of my life, for my help comes from you alone - Psalm 124:8.

2. My God and the only source of my help, let your help be readily available unto me in every issue and facet of my life in Jesus' name - Psm. 45:1; 121: 1, 2.

3. Oh God, my helper, let it be impossible for your help to elude me at any point-in-time of my life, in Jesus' name.

4. Oh God, my helper, by the reason of your powerful and resourceful help, turn my life around to your praise and to your glory.
5. Oh God, my help and shield, render your full help for my absolute change to come with an impenetrable security and shield for me against my foes and haters of my life – Psm. 33:20.
6. My God and helper, I pray that you make use of your Almighty power to make me and every human helper which you have predestined for my help from the foundations of the earth to come in contact with each other, in Jesus' name.
7. The Great I am that I am, I pray that you make use of the greatness of your power to locate my human helpers and forcefully direct them to me, to render the helps which you had ordained from your heavenly throne, in Jesus' name.
8. Oh my God, I decree the release of my human helpers from all contrary forces or satanic forces that are holding them down in any form of bondage from coming down to me, to do as you God has destined in Jesus' name.
9. Oh my God, I decree the removal of every veil and everything that the wicked have used to blindfold the physical eyes and the eyes of the mind of all my human helpers, which have hitherto made it impossible for them to be able to see me and be disposed to doing what is required of them to me as it had been ordained by you, in Jesus' name.

10. I decree that the eyes of understanding of all my God-ordained human helpers be enlightened, so that they can freely and liberally come to fulfill God's ideal in my life and towards my fulfillment in life, in Jesus' name.

11. Oh my God, by your power, influence every man, woman, male, female, young and old that you have ordained to be part of the fulfillment of every phase of my life to come to me at will and fulfill the mandate, in Jesus' mighty name.

12. Oh my help and shield, stop every mouth and satanic action from and through any individual person, people, peoples and organizations who might have stood and would want to stand against my being helped by those you have earmarked to do so to me, in the mighty name of Jesus Christ.

13. Oh my God, arise and scatter every force and operations of the wicked that stand between me and my helpers, from being able to render your God-ordained help to me, in Jesus' name.

14. Mighty God, by the instrumentality of your holy Angels, cause all my helpers in their various destinations all over the nations of the world to locate me and be drafted to me to do all your God-ordained will for me, in the mighty name of Jesus Christ.

15. All angelic entities, assigned for my help, take your full place and fully operate to render your sufficient helps to me, in the name of Jesus Christ.

16. I decree all Angelic beings assigned for my help, to go to every nook and cranny of the earth and bring helps for me and for my fulfillment, in Jesus' name.

17. Oh Great I am that I am, wherever human-helpers of my life are hiding or are maintaining a passive stand, locate, quicken and motivatedly bring them to me, to fulfill their God-ordained mandate in fully helping me, in Jesus' name.
18. Oh my God, empower and strengthen me to wait for your will, with reference to those you have ordained to be helpfully part of the fulfillment of your God-given mandate for my life in Jesus' name.
19. Oh God, grant me sufficient wisdom to relate with and wisely coordinate all the human-helpers that you bring on my way on this life voyage, in Jesus' name.
20. The great God of heavens and earth, empower me with godly habits and virtues that will enable me to maintain a Godly, life-fulfilling and hitch-free relationship with all my human-helpers, in Jesus' name.
21. Father God, raise proficient helpers for me, in all my endeavours as a Lawyer, a Minister of God, a Real Estate cum Properties Consultant, a Writer, a Publisher, a human right activist (mention your profession or trade) and bring them to me, to fulfill their helping-hand's mandate for my life, in Jesus name.
22. Oh my God, draw unto me, all persons, people and organizations that must work with me in every area, facet and phase of my endeavours, to enhance my fulfillment, in Jesus' name.
23. The Great I am that I am, enhance my fulfillment in Jesus' name.
24. My Father and my God, let it be impossible for my human helper to be directed to any other person, but to me, in Jesus' name.

25. Jehovah Elshadai God, cause my human helpers to targetedly come in contact with me and render help to me unto my fulfillment in life in Jesus' name.

26. Oh my God, Let and cause me to targetedly come in contact with my helpers, from all over the nations of the world, in Jesus' name.

27. Oh Mighty God, arise in my favour against every foe, detractors and fowlers who divert my human- helpers from coming to render their God-given mandate's help to me, in Jesus' name.

28. Oh God of my restoration, by the force of heaven, restore unto me my helpers who have been distracted and diverted from coming to me, hitherto, in Jesus' name.

29. Oh God of peace, restore peace between me and all my human-helpers, in Jesus' name

30. Jehovah God, by the blood of Jesus Christ, wipe out every mark, spot and blemish of my fowlers and wicked forces placed on me, that thus hinder my helper from reaching me and rendering God-ordained help for my life and destiny, in Jesus' name.

31. The Great I am that I am, remove every veil of the wicked placed upon my life, my career, business, books, office, sign-post and what have you in Jesus' name.

32. All the hosts of God's heavenly army, arise in your fierce anger and fury against the hosts of darkness, who stand between me, my helpers and God-ordained help that are meant to be rendered unto me; and scatter them, so that their help can be unfailingly rendered unto me, in Jesus name.

33. Jehovah God, cause an inseparable attachment to be the hallmark between me and your ordained human helpers for my life, in Jesus' name.

34. Jehovah God, cause a loving understanding which will put a permanent fusion between me and my human helpers to be our lot in Jesus' name.

35. I decree that there shall be no conflict and misunderstanding that will bring permanent separation between me and my human helpers, in Jesus' name.

36. I decree and declare unbreakable love for permanent and glorious relationship to exist between me and my human-helpers, in Jesus' name.

37. I scatter and destroy every gathering of the wicked that stand or arise against loving, fruitful and glorious relationship that is and should exist between me and my helpers in Jesus' name.

38. I decree destruction and command fire to burn every paraphernalia of darkness and wickedness that the wicked have put in place or are doing to severe me and my helpers, in Jesus' name.

39. I decree permanent separation and confusion to be set between my human helpers and all that are detracting them from me, in Jesus' name.

40. Oh God of heaven, cause your fruitful, protective and fulfilling covering to bind and be over me and my helpers, in Jesus' name.

41. Oh God cause an unhindered and established godly relationship between me and my human-helpers, in Jesus' name.

42. Father God, enrich all my human helpers, so that they shall not lack sufficient needs required to fulfill their mandate, in the ministry of help, given to them, particularly towards me, in Jesus' name.

43. I pray to you God that the dignity and honourable relationship that should be accorded to both my destiny helpers and I shall be the existing virtue between both parties, in Jesus' name.

44. Jehovah God, cause my destiny helpers to be a man, a woman, a male, a female, young or old people, organizations etc of honour and dignity and to maintain the same in life, in Jesus' name.

45. Father God, empower and engrace me sufficiently to maintain a life and lifestyle of honour, respect and dignity, in Jesus' name.

46. O Lord God, the ancient of days, enrich and bless my helpers and I with perfect help, sure protection and long life, in Jesus' name.

47. I receive unprecedented creative ability and wisdom for productive and fulfilling innovations and result for my helpers and I, in Jesus' name.

48. Father God, cause doors of riches, honour, glory, power and might to be opened to my human helpers and I, in Jesus name.

49. Oh God, engrace my helpers and I with selfless spirit and lifestyle, in Jesus' name.

50. Oh God of Glory, I receive the heart, spirit and grace for Glory of God to be the pivot of the works of my helpers and I, in Jesus' name.

CHAPTER NINE

Prayer for Structuring, Coordinating and Harnessingof Resources Unto Success

"To everything there is a season, and a time to every purpose under the heaven for there is a time for every purpose and for every work" (Eccl. 1:3, 17b).

Beloved reader, life is in phases. There is the starting time, called the beginning of life and the consummating time, called, the end of life. However, between the beginning and the end of life are stages and phases. Each of the phases has and is impregnated with goals that must be achieved.

In other words, there are what must be achieved at every stage or phase of life, in order for a person's beginning to be well established, all through, to an expected fulfilling and glorious end. It is for all these to become our lot that this prayer session is earmarked.

PRAYER POINTS

1. Father God, give unto me a redemptive and well established beginning in my life, ministry, career (mention your career), in Jesus' name.

2. I receive into my life, the spirit of wisdom, knowledge and understanding that will make my beginning in life to be established and my end in life to be fulfilled and glorious in Jesus' name.

3. I declare a hitch-free vision's execution for my life, from my beginning in life, unto its fulfilling end, in Jesus' name.

4. Oh God, open my understanding and enlighten me on what to do at every phase and or stage of my life, in order for my beginning to be okay, and for my end in life to be glorious, in Jesus' name.
5. Oh my Father and God, engrace and strengthen me, for me to be focused with discipline, in order for it to be easy for me to remain undistracted in my vision and its execution, from beginning unto the end.
6. God, I receive a resilient and ever enduring spirit that will enable me to persevere, until my glorious and fulfilling end in life is achieved.
7. I receive the grace to be fit to do what is expected of me, at every stage of my life in Jesus' name.
8. I receive the supply of all the wherewithal required, to be able to meet the needs of every stage of my life, unto my fulfilling end, in Jesus' name.
9. Oh God, establish my life with people and peoples from all walks of life locally and internationally, that must work and or be associated with me and my works/visions, in order for my end to have a safe landing.
10. Oh God, I receive the grace and strength for boldness, courage and controllable temperament in my voyage in life, from its beginning, through its end, in Jesus' name.
11. I receive in my life, the Spirit of the Lord, spirit of wisdom, knowledge, understanding and the fear of God to have a well established beginning through a glorious end in life, in the name of Jesus Christ.

12. I receive the spirit of grace to earness my resources together and prudently co-ordinate the various aspects of the phases of my life, from the beginning unto the end in the name of Jesus Christ.

13. Oh God of heaven, grant, and supply me all the resources: human, financial, material and real estates, among others that I need for glorious execution of my life's endeavour from the beginning to the end, in Jesus' name.
14. Oh God of heaven, grant unto me the wisdom to do what, where, when, with whom and how to do any particular thing at every stage or phase of my life, unto a glorious fulfilling end.
15. Oh my God, at the time of my marriage (for those who are yet to get married), which is another phase in a man or woman's life, lead me unto a suitable spouse that fits best into my life, in Jesus' name.
16. Oh my Father and my God, grant unto me the wisdom, ability and wherewithal to functionally play my role as a wife or as a husband in my matrimonial home (this prayer is also for yet to be married partner), in Jesus' name.
17. Oh God of heaven, establish my matrimonial home upon the rock of ages, for it to stand and never to fall all the days of my life, in Jesus' name.
18. Oh my God, I pray that you make my home and every member of us in the home a good success, in the name of Jesus Christ.

19. Oh mighty God, fortify my family as a whole and every individual member in the family with fire and power of the Holy Ghost in Jesus name.
20. Oh God of heaven and earth, make everyone in my family, a useful and responsible vessel unto you, unto humanity and unto the family, in Jesus' mighty name.
21. Oh God of glory, I pray that no one shall miss his or her phases in life, neither shall anyone fail in every of his or her phases, in the name of Jesus Christ.
22. I pray you, God of heaven, that none of us in my nuclear family and amongst every participant playing one role or the other in meeting my heavenly mandate on earth, shall lack or be in any want of what is required and needed at any point in time of the pursuit of the mandate unto its fulfillment, in the name of Jesus Christ.
23. God of glory, at the point of building my first living house and more, as well as building structures for: (1) My Ministries, Local Assembly or Church [for Ministering of the Gospel]; (2) Office or factory use, etc. lead me unto the location, finance me for the building construction unto finishing and be my shield and that of those who are favourably disposed towards me concerning the buildings, in the name of Jesus Christ.
24. Oh, Most High God, protect me and all that are favourably and progressively with me, from every form of hazards, casualties, marauding, assassina-tion and assassins. There shall be no loss of any in the name of Jesus Christ.

25. Oh Most High God, raise able workers and co-participants for me from every nations of the earth to make my fulfillment sure.
26. Oh God, open my understanding to the nitty-gritty of what to do unto accomplishment at every stage of my life, in Jesus' name
27. Oh Mighty God, cause me to do what is right and at your instance, at every stage of my life unto successful end.
28. My Father and my God, do not let me know shame, neither should shame come near me, in every stage of my life, in the name of Jesus Christ.
29. Father, remove everything that is, or that represents cankerworm, caterpillar, palmer worm and locust, in every aspect of my work, in any stage of my life, in the name of Jesus Christ.

30. Father God, cause every stage of my life to know unprecedented growth and global recognition to your glory and praise; in the name of Jesus Christ.

CHAPTER TEN

Prayer of Justification in Litigation and in Every Other Areas of My Life

"Therefore, there is now no condemnation - no adjudging guilty of wrong for those who are in Christ Jesus who live not after the dictates of the flesh, but after the dictates of the spirit" (Romans 8:1, Amplified Bible).

For:

"We have an Advocate (one who will intercede for us) with the Father, Jesus Christ the righteous" (1 John 2:1).

1. Oh my God and Justifier, justify me before all my opponents in physical, legal and spiritual tussles and cause my opponents to be fully condemned, in Jesus' name.

2. Present your case before God (Read Isaiah 44:2, 3, 6; 41:21a) and ask God to influence all the proceedings in your favour and against the opponents, in Jesus' name.
3. Lodge your complaints, in detail, to God against your petitioner(s) [mention name(s)], and those who are on his (their) side(s), e.g. relations, friends, counsel.
4. Make any requests that you have or want about them known unto God in earnest and fervent prayers.

5. Commit the heart(s) of the Judge (Justices), Magistrate or Lay Magistrate, Tribunal Panels, into God's hands, for Him to turn it (them) in your favour and justification. And of course, to the condemnation of your opponents.
6. Commit yourself, your counsel, his wisdom, preparation and utterance unto God.
7. Declare good concerning you, your counsel and your case.
8. Saturate the Court's premises and the Court where the suit is assigned with the blood of Jesus Christ, for sanctification, purification and refinery in Jesus' name.
9. Declare the blood of Jesus Christ to prevail for you against your opponent and his/her counsel.
10. Declare the atmosphere of any fixed date(s) free for the move of the Holy Spirit to influence the whole judicial processes and machinery favourably in your direction.
11. Nullify, render passive and destroy every diabolic or evil means that any of your opponent may use, have been using or want to use, in the mighty name of Jesus Christ.
12. Specifically, mention their counsel's name(s) and dis-arm him/her/them by breaking down his/her/their will power, confidence, and any means usable by him/her/them to counter your expectations for success as regards the case.
13. Frustrate your opponent's token and decree their diviners to turn mad (Isaiah 44:25-26).
14. Ask God to make your opponent's wisdom and that of their counsel become foolish.

15. Ask God to disappoint their crafty devices, so that their hands will not perform their enterprise (Job 5:12).
16. Ask God to catch them in their own craftiness.

17. Decree what you want and that which you do not want before, during and at the end of the matter, case or suit.
18. Bind all bindables and loose all loosables in the matter, in the name of Jesus Christ.
19. Declare your vindication from the realm of the spirit into the physical and legal realm.
20. Ask God to prove Himself to you as your justifier in the matter, for, "He is for you", so, "no one can be against you" (Rom. 8:31b).
21. Declare the Judge(s), magistrates, Members of Tribunal's spirit, soul and body to favour your cause and to be adverse to your opponent's cause, in Jesus' name.
22. Decree that your opponents, their counsel and those who are favourably disposed toward them shall not prosper. Rather, they shall be ashamed and be put into everlasting confusion, in Jesus' name.
23. Arise oh God and scatter all my opponents, be it in the spiritual realm, physical, soulical and legal, in the name of Jesus Christ.
24. God, embolden me and those who are with me, with the strength and wisdom of the Holy Spirit throughout the Court's proceedings for our success, in Jesus' name.
25. Mighty God, lead me and my Counsel on the way to follow, in the pursuit of this matter, for it to end up in

our success and favour, as against our opponents' matter, in the name of Jesus Christ.

26. Oh God my Justifier, cause an oversight to happen in the lives of the Judge, my opponents, their counsel and those who are on their side, that would favour my cause, in the name of Jesus Christ.

27. Oh God of host, terrorise my opponents, their Counsel and those who are with them, in such a way that they would loose their balance and bearing throughout the proceedings, in Jesus' name.

28. Oh my God, empower me so much that you would cause my opponents and all who are on their side to fall victim of their evil machinations against me, and let me witness their destructive end, in the name of Jesus' Christ.

29. Oh God my Father, cause me to be a beneficiary of the full benefits of the results of the case in my favour and in the favour of my client.

30. Warmly thank God with all your heart for answered prayers (1 John 5: 14).

Note: Please, after praying these prayers in truth and in spirit, cease from every form of anxiety and walk not by sight and by human senses (2 Cor. 5:7). Rather, have your complete rest in God, who is your faithful rewarder (Heb. 11:6c, 10:35, 36; Phil. 4:6, 7) and you will see the glory of God.

NOTICE: Order for a copy of a booklet, ***Prayer Pattern For Conquest*** by this same author and be totally free.

WHAT YOU MUST DO!

For your effort in prayer exercise with this book to be fruitful to you and not to be in futility, you must totally surrender and submit yourself to the LORDSHIP of JESUS CHRIST. You must be born again. How?

1st: Acknowledge your sins, that is, accept that you are a sinner and confess your sins to God in Jesus' name - 1 John 1:8, 9.

2nd: Acknowledge that you cannot save yourself

3rd: Acknowledge that Jesus Christ had been sent as your saviour and, as a propitiation for your sin - 2 Cor. 5:21; Act 4:12.

4th: Acknowledge that He shed His blood for the remission of your sins - Heb. 9:20, 28.

5th: Acknowledge that He died, but rose up the third day, from death for your justification - Rom. 4:24,25.

6th: Ask Him to come into your life as your Lord, to rule and reign over your life and affairs - Rev. 3:10.

7th: Believe that you have been forgiven, saved and you have received power to become a son or a daughter of God - Rom. 10:9-11; John 1:12, 13; Eph. 2:8, 9; Heb. 10:38, 39.

Other books by Samuel Jimson Olorunfemi:

- Supernatural Weapons for Believer's Deliverance
- Pray Till Something Happens
- 'Prayer' A 'Trust' (Stewardship in Prayer)
- Lifted Over the Devil in Victory
- Freedom For The Divorced
- Victory Over The Adamic Nature
- Quiet Time [Life-Long Tour With God] *(fast selling)*
- Akoko Idakeje
- Help From Above
- Breaking The Evil Blood Covenant
- Daily Spiritual Meal (Daily Devotional)
- Sunday School Manual for all Christians, Churches and Fellowships
- Victory In Your Zero Hour
- Golden Tips For Wealth and Riches
- From Convert To Spiritual Gianthood
- Way Out of Confusion
- Prayer Pattern For Conquest
- Wait on God Till Your Change Come

www.ingramcontent.com/pod-product-compliance
Lightning Source LLC
LaVergne TN
LVHW052053160826
845678LV00015B/3205

* 9 7 9 8 8 4 6 4 4 0 0 2 9 *